Freshwater Pond Animals

Biome Beasts

Lisa Colozza Cocca

ROURKE'S
SCHOOL to HOME
CONNECTIONS

BEFORE AND DURING READING ACTIVITIES

Before Reading: *Building Background Knowledge and Vocabulary*

Building background knowledge can help children process new information and build upon what they already know. Before reading a book, it is important to tap into what children already know about the topic. This will help them develop their vocabulary and increase their reading comprehension.

Questions and Activities to Build Background Knowledge:

1. Look at the front cover of the book and read the title. What do you think this book will be about?
2. What do you already know about this topic?
3. Take a book walk and skim the pages. Look at the table of contents, photographs, captions, and bold words. Did these text features give you any information or predictions about what you will read in this book?

Vocabulary: *Vocabulary Is Key to Reading Comprehension*

Use the following directions to prompt a conversation about each word.

- Read the vocabulary words.
- What comes to mind when you see each word?
- What do you think each word means?

Vocabulary Words:

- *arachnids*
- *barbels*
- *crustaceans*
- *glide*
- *hibernate*
- *lateral*
- *pharynx*
- *predators*
- *prey*
- *rooted*

During Reading: *Reading for Meaning and Understanding*

To achieve deep comprehension of a book, children are encouraged to use close reading strategies. During reading, it is important to have children stop and make connections. These connections result in deeper analysis and understanding of a book.

Close Reading a Text

During reading, have children stop and talk about the following:

- Any confusing parts
- Any unknown words
- Text to text, text to self, text to world connections
- The main idea in each chapter or heading

Encourage children to use context clues to determine the meaning of any unknown words. These strategies will help children learn to analyze the text more thoroughly as they read.

When you are finished reading this book, turn to the next-to-last page for **Text-Dependent Questions** and an **Extension Activity**.

Table of Contents

Biomes....4
Life at the Bottom....7
Life in the Middle....12
Life at the Edges....17
Life at the Surface....23
Activity: Water Tension Experiment....29
Glossary....30
Index....31
Text-Dependent Questions....31
Extension Activity....31
About the Author....32

Biomes

A biome is a large region of Earth with living things that have adapted to the conditions of that region.

A pond biome is a body of fresh, still water surrounded by land. It is usually less than seven feet (two meters) deep. Sunlight usually reaches the bottom, where most pond plants are **rooted**.

The temperature throughout a pond is about the same as the air temperature. In cold areas, ponds sometimes freeze solid.

Ponds exist around the world in all kinds of climates. Some plants and animals can live within one pond biome, but not in another because of the climate of its region.

Life at the Bottom

Many fish, **crustaceans**, and insects live in the muddy bottom of the pond. The bottom gets more crowded in cold winters, when ponds freeze over. Frogs and turtles **hibernate** in the mud during the cold season.

frog hibernating

Did You Know?

Crayfish, sometimes called crawdaddies, are a kind of crustacean. They hide under rocks and logs at the pond's bottom. They are nocturnal hunters that eat snails, bugs, worms, tadpoles, and plants.

Water scorpions are insects. Unlike true scorpions, they are not **arachnids**. Water scorpions walk along the bottom of the pond and hide among dead leaves there. Their front legs have adapted to catch other bugs and small fish.

The water scorpion has a long, thin tail that sticks up out of the water. The tail is made up of two long tubes that act like a snorkel, so the bug can breathe while underwater.

Catfish are also bottom dwellers. On hot days, catfish stay cool in holes in the mud or under logs or rocks on the pond floor. They are most active at night when they hunt for insects, plants, crayfish, snails, and algae to eat.

snail

Their **barbels**, which look like cat whiskers, are made of skin. They contain taste buds and the fish's sense of smell. They help catfish locate **prey** in the dark.

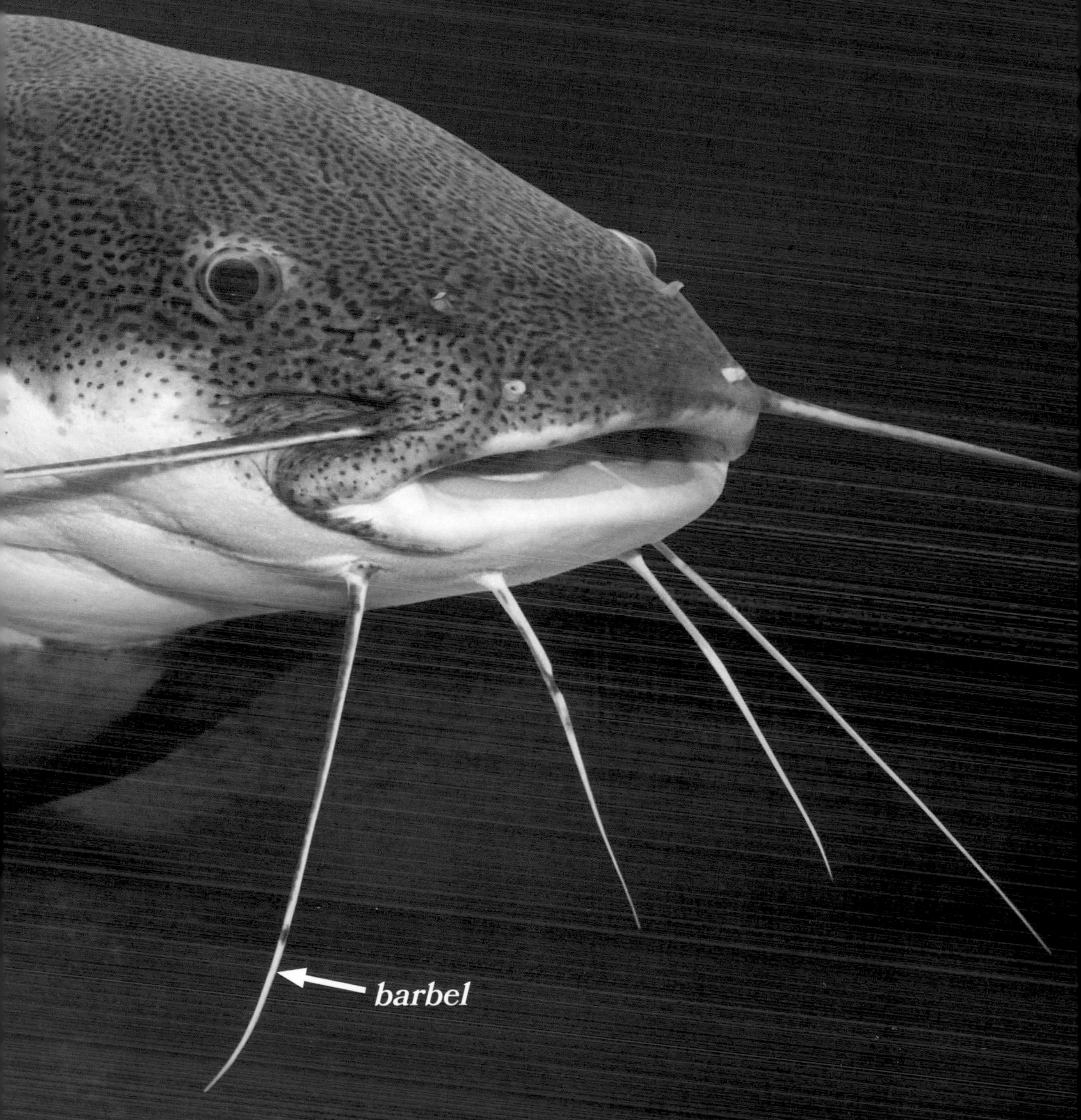

barbel

Life in the Middle

Some amphibians, such as frogs, toads, and newts, hatch in the middle of ponds. The area is also home to lots of insects. Giant water bugs, water beetles, and caddis flies live there.

newt

Did You Know?

Plankton, tiny plant and animal life forms, float in the middle of the pond. Plankton is a food source for many pond animals.

western pond turtle

The western pond turtle nests on land, but spends most of its time in water. The water protects it from land **predators**, such as raccoons and coyotes. However, water predators, such as birds, fish, and bullfrogs, are still a danger. They eat young turtles that haven't formed hard shells yet. Adult turtles can pull their heads and legs inside their shells for extra protection.

Many fish, such as largemouth bass, live in the middle area of a pond. Young bass eat plankton, while adults eat fish, frogs, bugs, and even small birds. These fish have a sixth sense, called a **lateral** line, that picks up vibrations in water. This helps bass locate prey. The largemouth bass can eat prey up to one-fourth its body length.

Did You Know?

The largemouth bass is usually the biggest fish in the pond, so predators are not a problem.

The bluegill is a tall, flat sunfish. Its shape allows it to zigzag through the pond at great speed. Predators have difficulty following and catching it.

Tiny hair cells in its inner ear and a lateral line help the bluegill locate prey. The bluegill quickly opens its small mouth and expands its **pharynx**, a space behind its nostrils and mouth. It sucks up water into this space with the prey trapped inside.

Life at the Edges

Some animals live along the edges of ponds. Water snakes swim in these shallow waters to hunt for fish, frogs, and toads. In warm weather, the snakes often go on land. In cold winters, they burrow into the muddy bottom to keep warm.

Did You Know?

Water snakes hang from tree branches that stretch over the pond. This position gives them an easy escape from land predators. The snakes just drop into the pond when in danger!

Great blue herons are large wading birds with long legs and necks. Specially shaped bones in the bird's neck allow it to thrust its sharp beak very quickly into the water to catch fish.

Did You Know?

Fingernail clams have top and bottom shells that are joined at one end. Special sensors help this tiny mollusk stay top-up in the water.

Beavers and water shrews are rodents that live in ponds. The beaver's webbed back feet make it better at swimming than walking.

The beaver builds its den along the pond banks. It cuts down trees with its sharp teeth. Its front paws carry mud and other building supplies. The den has only one entrance, which is underwater below the freeze line.

Did You Know?

In fall, beavers store logs in the muddy bottom of a pond. When the pond freezes, they swim out of their dens and down to the underwater cafeteria to eat the stored logs.

The water shrew nests in a tunnel or under a log near a pond. The stiff hairs on its feet trap air bubbles. This allows the shrew to walk on water.

The water shrew's fur is lined with a layer of air. The layer slows heat loss and makes the shrew float in water. The water shrew must paddle hard with its large hind feet to dive below the surface.

Life at the Surface

Birds and bugs swim on the pond surface. Wood ducks have a round body shape that makes them float higher than other ducks in the water. They use their webbed feet to paddle. Claws on their feet allow the ducks to perch in branches when out of the pond.

Young wood ducks eat insects and small fish. Adults are plant eaters. They eat from the pond surface or dip their heads underwater. Sometimes the ducks even flip upside down to grab food underwater.

female wood duck with ducklings

Did You Know?

Male wood ducks are known for their beautiful colors. Females are brown and gray. When in danger, ducklings hide under their mother's wings. The females' plain coloring helps protect them from predators.

The American coot looks like a duck in water, but like a chicken on land. It has large feet with long toes that have scale-covered flaps on them.

Its short, rounded wings make it difficult for the bird to take flight. The coot scrambles across the water's surface while flapping its wings hard and fast to take off. Once in the air, it can fly easily.

The American coot's predators include osprey, bald eagles, and snapping turtles. Escaping them is difficult because the coot needs a running start to take off. Instead, the coot makes loud noises and splashes water to scare off the predator.

The water strider has tiny hairs on its six legs that trap air so it can walk or **glide** on the water. Its short front legs catch and hold prey, such as mosquitoes and dragonflies. Water striders live about a year in warm areas. In areas with cold winters, they die at the first freeze.

Did You Know?

The water strider is also known as a pond skater because of the way it glides across the pond's surface.

Ponds are busy places. Found around the world, each freshwater pond biome is home to a variety of living things that have adapted to the conditions in that particular place.

ACTIVITY: Water Tension Experiment

Have you wondered how some insects and animals skitter across water without sinking into it? The answer is surface tension. A barrier forms across the top of the water when only air is above it because of the force that pulls water molecules together. Try this experiment to learn more about how surface tension works.

Supplies

- four bowls
- water
- ground black pepper
- toothpick
- liquid soap
- unused, opened staple
- two 2-inch (5.08-centimeter) squares of lightweight foil

Directions

1. Fill bowls with water.
2. Shake pepper onto the surface of the water in the first bowl. What happens?
3. Coat the end of the toothpick with liquid soap.
4. Gently touch the surface of the water with the toothpick. What happens?
5. In the second bowl, gently place the staple on top of the water. What happens?
6. Repeat steps 3 and 4. What happens?
7. In the third bowl, gently lay one square of foil on top of the water. What happens?
8. Crush the remaining piece of foil into a tight ball. Place it on top of the water in the fourth bowl. What happens?

Think about how the soap broke the surface tension in the water. Did the pepper and staple sink or move away from the break? Think about how the balled foil acted differently than the flat foil. What does that tell you about animals that cross the water without breaking the tension?

Glossary

arachnids (uh-RAK-nids): arthropods with no backbone, eight legs, and no antennae, such as spiders, scorpions, and ticks

barbels (BAHR-buhls): thin growths on the heads of some fish that hold some of the fish's senses

crustaceans (kruh-STAY-shuhns): water animals with an outer shell, such as lobsters or crabs

glide (glide): to move smoothly with little effort

hibernate (HYE-bur-nate): to go into a deep sleep in which heart rate and breathing slow down, and body temperature drops

lateral (LAT-ur-uhl): from, by, on, or to the side

pharynx (FER-ingks): a space that connects the nose and mouth to the tube that leads to the stomach

predators (PRED-uh-turs): animals that hunt other animals for food

prey (pray): an animal that is hunted by another animal for food

rooted (ROO-ted): fixed in a particular place by roots

Index

American coot 25, 26
beaver(s) 19, 20
fish('s) 7, 8, 11, 13, 14, 17, 18, 24
great blue herons 18
water scorpion(s) 8, 9
water shrew(s) 19, 21, 22
water snakes 17
water strider(s) 27
western pond turtle 13
wood duck(s) 23, 24

Text-Dependent Questions

1. Why can a water shrew float?
2. How does a water scorpion breathe underwater?
3. How does the shape of a bluegill's body protect it from predators?
4. Why is it important for the entrance to a beaver's den to be under the water's surface?
5. How do the short, rounded wings of an American coot affect the bird's safety?

Extension Activity

Work with friends to develop a plan to protect ponds in your community. Write a letter to community leaders explaining why ponds are important. Include the plan you developed.

About the Author

Lisa Colozza Cocca has enjoyed reading and learning new things for as long as she can remember. She lives in New Jersey by the coast and loves wiggling her toes in the edge of a pond. You can learn more about Lisa and her work at www.lisacolozzacocca.com.

www.rourkeeducationalmedia.com

PHOTO CREDITS: Cover, page 1: ©VDV; ©davemhuntphotography; graphics: ©LEOcrafts; page 4: ©ollo; page 5: ©Rike_; page 6 (a): ©sankai; page 6 (b): ©DenisTangneyJr; page 6 (c): ©efesenko; page 6 (d): ©Lisa Bronitt; page 7: ©marefoto; pages 8-9: ©ElSnow; pages 10-1: ©abadonian; page 10: ©lauriek; page 12: ©scacciamosche; page 13: ©Sekar Balasubramanian; page 14: ©Joe Potato; page 15: ©Grant 77; page 16: ©Willard; page 18: ©Clark42; page 19: ©sebastien lemyre; page 20 (a): ©szymonbartosz.pl; page 20 (b): ©OGphoto; page 20 (c): ©Stanley45; page 21: ©MikeLane45; page 22: ©Rudmer Awerver; page 23: ©pchoui; page 24 (a): ©Lynn_Bystrom; page 24 (b): ©jmci; page 25: ©BrianLasenby; page 26: ©Jackal Photography; page 24: ©MarkMirror; page 28: ©IPGGutenbergUKLtd; pages 28-32: ©PhotoboyKO

Edited by: Kim Thompson
Cover design by: Kathy Walsh
Interior design by: Rhea Magaro-Wallace

Library of Congress PCN Data

Freshwater Pond Animals / Lisa Colozza Cocca
(Biome Beasts)
ISBN 978-1-73161-443-8 (hard cover)
ISBN 978-1-73161-238-0 (soft cover)
ISBN 978-1-73161-548-0 (e-Book)
ISBN 978-1-73161-653-1 (ePub)
Library of Congress Control Number: 2019932143

Rourke Educational Media
Printed in the United States of America,
North Mankato, Minnesota